D0174300

Praise for
The Future of Omni-Channel Retail

A well-distilled volume processing the past, present and future of consumption. Want a good quick read? It's right here.

Paco Underhill
Author of *Why We Buy: The Science of Shopping*

This concise, readable book describes why a growing portion of e-commerce belongs to traditional retailers who are moving online, and an increasing amount of brick-and-mortar sales belong to online companies moving to Main Street. It provides the statistics on how over-stored America has become, and how certain retailers are successfully competing against Amazon. One fascinating development he details are online services helping traditional stores to compete, by giving them a "long tail on the web." Traditional stores can discover how to best utilize the array of channels to them by asking, "What job is the consumer hiring them to do?" If you are a retailer, a supplier to retailers, an investor, or a real estate professional, there is something here for you.

Kent Trabing
Director of Real Estate, True World Group

Lionel Binnie's, *The Future of Omni-Channel Retail*, is a little book with a BIG idea. In fact, Binnie's principal concept is to offer an insightful, easy to understand, and easy to use framework for navigating through the piles of information and opinions on how to provide products and services to our customers in the future. The book's small size makes it perfectly suitable to serve as a guidebook that retailers and those interested in the sector will want to keep always available and close at hand.

Henry Welt
Co-Founder, Ossining Innovates! Former CEO Van Cleef & Arpels

The act of purchasing fulfills different consumer goals and needs. I think Mr. Binnie does an excellent job in explaining consumer purchase considerations and behavior. Understanding buyer behavior, combined with knowing retail history, helps us predict the future of retailing. I believe his insights provide a view of the future.

Milton J. Sussberg
Adjunct Professor of Entrepreneurship, Fordham University
President, Sussberg & Co., Inc.

For the decades I have known and worked with Lionel Binnie, he has always had a strategic perspective on the retail market in all its variations. His innovations and insights have produced great results for his clients. In his book, *The Future of Omni-Channel Retail*, Binnie explains how the Discovery and Fulfillment steps of marketing are pervasive yet unique across the many channels of our retail landscape. Developing an understanding of how to leverage the unique qualities of each channel is crucial for every omni-channel retailer and Binnie's book will help you do just that.

John Hessell
Former CEO, with 40 years in Specialty Retail

I have had the pleasure of knowing Lionel Binnie for two decades in several capacities: client, consultant, business partner and friend. He is a master of channel marketing and retail. I've learned many things from Lionel about brands, merchandising and intercepting the consumer with occasion and impulse buying. I am not only glad he is sharing his thoughts, intellect and insights in his inaugural book *The Future of Omni-Channel Retail*, but I feel privileged to have had the opportunity to read an advance copy. Anyone venturing into retail and e-commerce today would be wise to read what Lionel has written in the pages of this book. You'll be wiser and smarter for it. I know I am.

John J. Eccleston
Sr. Director of Brands Development for a Fortune 150 company,
brands maven, business entrepreneur and author

The Future of Omni-Channel Retail

Predictions in the Age of Amazon

Lionel Binnie

EMERALD LAKE
BOOKS

*To my father Michael and mother Carol,
who filled our childhood home
with books and a love of reading.*

Contents

Introduction

A new medium is never an addition to an old one,
nor does it leave the old one in peace. It never
ceases to oppress the older media until it finds new
shapes and positions for them.

Marshall McLuhan

When we can order almost anything online, will we? That's the future that is rapidly becoming our present. In a one-day or even two-hour home-delivery world, what types of experiences will still entice consumers to shop in-store? Will there even be any shops left to browse in if we still wanted to? If so, what types of shops?

Jim Cramer, an analyst on the business channel CNBC, once said, "Younger consumers don't want to go out. They just want to order food on Grubhub so they can stay on their couch and keep playing 'Call of Duty.'" He was saying that the move to online shopping is accelerating. People, especially those under 35, don't want to leave home if they don't have to, and businesses that make this possible are everywhere.

E-commerce has been with us for more than twenty years. Yet we are in an interesting time now because we can see the developing relationship between online shopping and physical, brick-and-mortar stores. The fog is starting to lift. The emerging shapes of online and offline retailing, as well as the ways they're likely to develop and interact, are becoming clearer than ever before. It's an exciting time, with great possibilities coming into view. Perhaps for the first time, greater clarity than ever before is available to us.

The term "omni-channel" has emerged in the retail industry to refer to this new blend of online and offline retail. "Omni" comes from the Latin *omnis* meaning "all," and "channel" comes from the Latin *canalis* meaning "canal." Channel is an often-used business metaphor to explain how products flow down a distribution channel from their source through various stages and businesses to the consumer.

The diagram to the right illustrates how the different pieces work together.

"Omni-channel," "omnichannel" or "omni channel" are used interchangeably by marketing experts, but we'll use "omni-channel" throughout this narrative.

Let's not get sidetracked by terminology, though. Whatever we call it, we are clearly in an era where retailing has forever changed. In this book, I take a close look at this developing retail landscape to

examine which paths are most clear, and how far down some of those paths we can see at this time.

As a consumer products and food marketer, I've spent years peering into that fog, observing as these larger shapes emerge from the mist. I've been asking myself:

- Where is all this going?
- What can we say for sure about where internet retail is heading as the mist lifts?
- What can we be certain about?
- What is still unclear?
- What should our responses be as business thinkers and actors in this $5 trillion industry (total annual U.S. retail sales)?
- How are online and offline channels playing off one another?
- What will omni-channel retail look like going forward?
- To what extent will different product categories move further online?
- Which product categories will move the furthest online, and why?
- What product attributes and buying occasions are factors influencing whether products are more likely to be purchased online?
- What types of product categories will continue to rely on an offline brick-and-mortar presence?
- With this in mind, what types of offline shopping environments (malls, stores, shopping centers, downtowns, etc.) will still be viable in the foreseeable future?

- What characteristics will help those offline shopping experiences and environments remain viable?
- What is it about offline, tangible shopping that is least replaceable by online shopping? (Hint— think discovery, social experience, community building, dining, services, entertainment).

In my career, I've spent the last three decades working at the intersection of consumer product and food marketing, distribution, wholesaling and retailing. I have managed and selected malls and spaces within malls for over 200 holiday kiosks selling gift products throughout the U.S. I have observed people's shopping behavior up close.

Later, as a business development strategist at iZone Group, a national distributor of fashion eyewear and accessories, I was responsible for getting our sunglasses and other fashion products in front of as many consumers as possible. In this role, I developed new channels of distribution, first in highway travel plazas and then in airports, nationally.

I realized that it was important to get these products not only in front of crowds, but also crowds that were in the right frame of mind to buy. I thought long and hard about the role of location and timing for the optimal placement of products in the U.S. retail market.

When I became a consultant, I repeated the exercise with Cejon, which was acquired by Steve Madden, helping them enter the Canadian market and highway travel venues. I was also a partner in a business that sold fashion scarves and accessories in college bookstores nationwide, and operated pop-up shops and events to promote those products.

More recently I've worked with consumer and food brands

to help them open distribution in other high-traffic venues favorable to consumer sales and branding, such as large colleges, hospitals, corporate workplaces and travel venues.

What these different projects have had in common has been the overarching questions: What works? What is optimal? In getting a product in front of consumers, where are the best locations to place products? What is the right convergence between the product, customer and venue?

You could say I'm a placement expert, a connoisseur of product placement opportunities, a "place whisperer" even— someone who teases out the right questions and answers that lead to optimal product placements.

When those placement opportunities have been identified, I've also developed the business muscles, techniques and connections with the various channel partners who provide access. What types of partnerships need to be developed to obtain this "sweet spot" distribution, where it all comes together?

From my vantage point as an industry participant and an intensely curious person, I've closely observed the development of omni-channel retail. The blending of technology with retail and the evolution of various e-commerce business models that have come and gone (flash sales anyone?) have fascinated me. I am awed by the potential of e-commerce to make the physical placement of products in the real world obsolete.

To revisit my opening question, when we can order virtually anything online and have it delivered to our front door, will we ever still want to shop in an offline world? Ultimately, will viewing a product on a screen and reading other buyers' reviews of the product be enough for us to stay home for many, or even most, shopping occasions?

How will this ubiquity of product information and availability that the internet offers affect how, when and where we still will want to shop in person and experience the entertaining and social aspect of shopping in stores, markets, malls, arcades and on the street? And if we do still want to, why will we want to when we don't have to? The answer might surprise you.

You may be astonished to hear that some of the promises of digital distribution and online retail have begun to fall short and reverse themselves, such as the rise and present decline in use of eReaders (Kindle, Nook and tablets), and the re-emergence of independent bookstores.[1]

It turns out that the structure and charm of physical books are not entirely replaced by words on a screen. The phenomenon of screen fatigue is becoming more readily apparent, causing consumers to return to the simple pleasure of reading books and magazines in print. Add to that the essence of brick-and-mortar bookstores as places of charm, social interaction and discovery, and there is a certain gravitational pull that makes browsing, buying and reading books in a store, a delight.

You also may be surprised to learn that new online brands like Warby Parker (eyewear), Casper (mattresses) and Harry's Razors have all learned that they still need a presence in physical stores to maximize their reach. These businesses have discovered that online-only is a limited and limiting strategy. Stores as a means of consumer discovery and fulfillment, still work, and work well.

This book consists of three parts. The first part, Chapter 1, is a somewhat quick and playful glance back through history to see how we got here. It provides a very brief tour through the history of human exchange and retail, noting the different disruptions along the way. This is to help us to zoom out and gain some helpful perspective on where we currently are.

The next part consists of Chapters 2 through 4, and tackles the present era. Chapter 2 looks at our current period of retail disruption and examines its fundamental nature, while Chapter 3 reviews current marketing models of shopping behavior and brings them together into my own two-axis model. This model can be used to plot any product type and shopping occasion to predict which ones will likely move further toward online shopping. For those that are more resistant to this change, I also delve into the reasons for that resistance. After that, Chapter 4 explores the current state of retail disruption, where we examine retail store and shopping mall closings as well as the re-purposing of real estate that has already occurred. This chapter also analyzes food retailing and the restaurant industry, along with the move toward fresher food and home delivery models.

In the final part, Chapter 5, I look at key aspects of omnichannel retail and make predictions about where these trends are likely to go in the future, based on my two-axis predictive model.

Are you with me? Let's dive in!

Part I. The Past

Chapter 1.

How We Got Here
(A Quick Tour of Retail History)

Retail disruption has always been around. What this chapter and the timeline image at the end of it lack in detail, they make up for in perspective. The point of the exercise is to zoom out and view our current situation in the context of the last twenty years or so, and then locate that era within the perspective of history. Change, development and, yes, that over-used word "disruption," are nothing new. What *is* new is the speed and scale of the current disruptions.

Out of the mists of pre-history, our hunter-gatherer ancestors emerged. Before 10,000 BC, the gathering of nuts, fruits and other plants, as well as the hunting of game, were the pre-economic survival activities of our ancestors. It was pre-commerce. You

gathered or hunted your food and perhaps shared with your clan, maybe trading apples for nuts or goats for chickens. Pretty straightforward.

Around 10,000 BC, humans developed agriculture. Yuval Harari, in his fascinating book *Sapiens—A Brief History of Humankind*, delves deeply into how farming developed and explores some of its more colorful details. For example, the first crops to be cultivated were wheat, the first animals to be domesticated were probably goats, and agriculture first developed in the Middle East, China and central America. Why? Because that's where easily farmed crops, like rice and wheat, and easily herded animals, like goats and cows, already naturally existed. There are relatively few plant and animal species that were readily domesticated.

Interestingly, Harari makes the strong case that humans were actually better off as hunter-gatherers and that there were real drawbacks to the rise of agriculture. For example, the specialization farming required resulted in a much more restricted range of foods for the farmer, leading to less varied and therefore less healthy diets. Additionally, the surpluses created by agriculture resulted in social classes and the exploitation of laborers by landowners. It also led to an increase in violence, which was required to defend (or capture) precious land, now a source of security, from other tribes.

But there was no going back. The increased populations that agriculture created could never have been sustained in a hunter-gatherer system anyway—too much land was required. But back to our history.

Agriculture allowed people to extract more food from much less land than hunting and gathering. That allowed for population growth. It also resulted in specialization and exchange. For example, I might focus on raising wheat, while you might raise chickens. I'd then have surplus grain and you'd have extra birds. This means we could exchange. So, agriculture directly resulted in exchange and bartering, haggling over how many chickens a bag of wheat is worth.

Simplifying Commerce

After another 9,000 years, at around 1,000 BC, the concept of money evolved.

Money doesn't necessarily mean metal discs or paper notes. It's any accepted medium of exchange that means I don't have to take what you have in surplus and trade it for my surplus. Essentially, an accepted medium allows me to turn an excess of anything valuable into something else.

There are many limitations of barter. I always need to find someone who values what I have in excess—say, apples—and who also has an excess of what I need—say, shoes. So, the development of money dramatically freed up commerce. It allowed for the development of a greater variety of goods and services being produced and exchanged. One person could focus on making great shoes, another on baking the best bread, and another on crafting really cool chairs—more and better stuff.

The types of money varied by culture. Sometimes it was just a predetermined portion of barley, but it could also be shells or beads. Later, imprinted metal coins were developed around 700 BC, which were sanctioned by the political authority that guaranteed the coins' value, which also was an important factor in facilitating commerce.

Another result of agriculture and its capacity for exchange was the development of towns and cities. The greater efficiency of farming meant more food could be extracted from the same land as gathering and hunting, resulting in greater population density. These greater concentrations of people allowed for more efficient exchanges of surplus farming products and other goods.

Now that we've got concentrations of people, more variety of goods, and an efficient and trusted way to buy them, what's missing? The mall! (But more on malls later…)

The Development of Shopping

Archaeological evidence exists of early shops and markets in what is now modern-day Iran and Turkey from 7,000 to 6,000 BC. In ancient Greece, the central communal space of the town, the Agora, was used as a market on particular days. In ancient Rome, the forum was the communal central space of the city. Permanent buildings were created there to house shops. These may have been the earliest permanent shopping centers in history. Trajan's forum, which still exists in Rome, was a four-story building housing permanent shops.

In northern Africa and western Asia, the name still used for a central market is *souk* (in Arabic) or in Persian, *bazaar*. Dating back to 600 BC, these central markets are still to be found, usually in the old central parts of cities in this part of the world. They were located where the caravans came into town, bringing goods for exchange from other regions, and later they became permanent. Besides commerce, they had a social function, where people could interact, and a cultural function, where culture, art, crafts, music and poetry were exchanged. We will come back to these extra-commercial functions of the market later in the book.

Jumping forward, markets proliferated in medieval Europe. Records show that in 1516, England had 2,464 markets. The local lord would grant a charter to a market for a fee, guaranteeing that another competing market could not operate on the same day. Markets operated weekly or bi-weekly and were supplemented by annual fairs that celebrated religious holidays. The fair was an occasion for a temporary market that offered a greatly expanded array of merchandise.

Larger cities had areas where different craftsmen had workshops where they produced goods like metal-work, carpentry, leather, pottery and textiles, as well as foodstuffs and taverns.

These were supplemented by market days in a central market square, where farmers from neighboring areas would bring in their agricultural products.

In the age of discovery and colonization in the Middle Ages, European adventurers brought back goods from Asia and the Americas, opening up new opportunities for trade and many new products that offered retail opportunities and expanded product selections in markets. Tomatoes came from the Andes and potatoes from what is now Peru in South America. Spices came from the tropics. These new foods and products transformed and expanded markets in Europe.

Medieval markets were followed by better markets in spaces specifically designed for the purpose, like the Galeries Du Bois[2] created in the 1770s. Inspired by the forums of ancient Rome and the souks of Arabia, the Galeries Du Bois was a shopping arcade located in Paris in the square around the royal palace. It became more than just a place of commerce. It was the artistic, social and political center of Paris at the time, consisting of a collection of stores, galleries, bookshops, cafés and restaurants. It attracted aristocrats, intellectuals, students and business-people and was an escape from the smells, hubbub and chaos of central Paris.

In the nineteenth century, department stores were developed, first in Europe and then in the U.S. The origin of the department store is in some dispute, as many of the earliest operators were inspired by one another.

One of the earliest true department stores, Le Bon Marche, was developed by the French fabric salesman Aristide Boucicaut around 1850. Inspired by his experience visiting the World's Fair, Boucicaut's intention was to create a sensory overload for the consumer. Boucicaut called his store a "cathedral of commerce" that offered a "spectacle of extraordinary proportions, so that going to the store became an event, an adventure."[3] He employed the engineer Gustave Eiffel (of the Eiffel Tower) and the latest technology in cast iron and glass to create huge skylights, letting natural light into the enormous 3-story, almost 600,000 square foot building.

Other early department stores following the same model were Bainbridge's in London, followed by Harrods.

A.T. Stewart, an Irish immigrant to the U.S., who became one of the twenty wealthiest people in history ($90B in U.S. today's dollars), founded his Marble Palace, an early American department store in New York City in 1848.

Around this time, some of the earliest omni-channel retail experiments also began. Instantaneous communication via the telegraph was invented in 1844 and was in widespread use by the 1860s. In Steven Spielberg's movie "Lincoln," there is a scene in which President Lincoln is communicating practically in real time with his generals on the front line by telegraph. When you combine this with the fast and efficient transportation provided by railroads, also being perfected and expanded in the mid-19th century, and the printing of an enormous catalogue of goods (Sears), the possibility of ordering a product and receiving it in just a couple of days came into being. In reality, consumer orders were likely placed by mail rather than by telegraph, but the potential for e-commerce was foreshadowed in this era. It was the technologies and systems of secure mail combined with railroads that made mail-order retail businesses viable in the mid-19th century.

Leveraging the new rapid and secure transportation provided by railroads, and the reliable mail system of the Penny Post made the first mail-order business possible. It was founded in 1861 in Wales, in the U.K., by Pryce Pryce-Jones. He shipped locally-produced flannel fabrics around the U.K. and later sold an early form of sleeping bag he invented.

In the U.S., Montgomery Ward's catalog began in 1872, followed by Sears and Roebuck in '93. They started with watches and went on to sell virtually everything imaginable in their vast catalogs. But it was 32 years before Sears even opened their first store in 1925. By that time, more catalogs appeared for every type of merchandise, from Hammacher Schlemmer (tools) to L.L. Bean and Land's End (outdoor gear and apparel).

As the television era developed in the second half of the 20th century, this became another shopping avenue. TV home shopping reached its apex in the 1980s with channels like the Home Shopping Network and QVC.

The Origin Story of the Enclosed Shopping Mall

The origin of the U.S. shopping mall is worth looking at in some detail in our history of retail, so we'll now make a small detour to take a closer look at this important business and cultural phenomenon.

If we must trace the origin of the U.S. shopping mall to one person, it would be the Austrian architect Victor Gruen (1903-1980). Gruen was born and raised in Vienna, and studied architecture at the Vienna Academy of Fine Arts, opening his own firm in 1933. But after the Nazis annexed Austria in 1938, he emigrated first to England and then to the U.S. "with an architect's degree, eight dollars and no English."[4]

His early U.S. projects involved designing innovative storefronts for shops on 5th Avenue in New York City in the 1940s. These pioneering retail designs showed a clever understanding of shopper psychology in that they had open frontages designed to entice pedestrians to walk into the store off the street, without necessarily planning to.

His first enclosed shopping center project was Southdale Mall in Edina, Minnesota, in 1954.

This was hailed as a dramatic and positive modernization that attracted national media attention. *Life* magazine called it "the splashiest center in the U.S." While *Time* magazine called it a "pleasure-dome-with-parking."

What was new about it was that it was an entirely enclosed system of shops with no exterior windows and a climate-controlled interior. This was a particularly good fit for Minnesota with its cold winters. Until then, shops in malls and arcades were connected by outside walkways. This new design was on two levels, had a department store at each end, and escalators to bring shoppers up to the second level and down again when they'd completed walking the mall. And it had a central court with skylights, fountains, plants and seating.

Gruen was inspired by the centrally planned urban re-development of his hometown of Vienna, Austria, that took place because of the democratic uprisings in 1848.

Malcolm Gladwell, in his article "The Terrazzo Jungle" in the *New Yorker* magazine, describes these Viennese developments:

> The Parliament now faced directly onto the street. The walls that separated the élite of Vienna from the unwashed in the suburbs were torn down. And, most important, a ring road, or Ringstrasse—a grand mall—was built around the city, with wide sidewalks and expansive urban views, where Viennese of all backgrounds could mingle freely on their Sunday afternoon stroll. To the Viennese reformers of the time, the quality of civic life was a function of the quality of the built environment, and Gruen thought that principle applied just as clearly to the American suburbs.[5]

Gruen's mall concept was really a synthetic version of the old downtown shopping areas of many American towns. With a couple of department stores and many smaller shops and restaurants in between.

The problem, from a business optimization viewpoint, was these downtown shopping areas were unplanned. Besides the fact that they were outside, making the weather a factor, the layout couldn't be fully controlled since the buildings were owned by different landlords. There was no central control of leasing—you couldn't create adjacencies to maximize sales. For example, having a men's shoe store next to a men's clothing store or a jewelry store next to a dress shop to stimulate additional sales by attracting the same type of customer.

Gruen's centrally planned enclosed shopping mall solved all these issues by having a single landlord who could organize and lease the entire mall to optimize the shopping experience. These malls were intended to positively impact the surrounding community and be integrated into it. That meant they weren't just intended to contain stores, but would also include housing, schools, museums and parks.

What happened instead, to Gruen's later disapproval, was the endless replication of his enclosed mall design. Instead of being parts of larger thoughtful developments, they were simply thrown up into the middle of former farmland on the edges of suburbs where land was the cheapest.

Worse yet, because shoppers had to drive to get there, malls were surrounded by acres of unattractive parking lots instead of being integrated into a larger holistic community. Nothing could have been farther from what Gruen envisioned when he designed that first indoor mall.

A Blow to Main Street

Before suburban shopping malls stole business from the old downtown department stores and main streets, there were multiple family-owned regional department stores throughout the U.S. and each region and major city had their own, including Hecht's in Baltimore, L.S. Ayres in Indianapolis, Donaldson's in Minneapolis, and Macy's in New York.

But the suburban enclosed malls disrupted entire cities. They drew business, vitality and traffic from the old downtowns and Main Streets to the developing suburbs, where the parents of the Baby Boomer generation wanted to live.

In the 1980s and '90s, Walmart and other Big Box stores returned the favor, grabbing traffic from both malls and Main Streets. Consumer traffic moved to the large strip centers anchored by Big Box stores, oftentimes relocating even farther out in the suburbs, where the cheapest land was, especially in the small towns of America. Walmart was the Amazon of its day, decimating the local merchants of Main Street and later the local grocery stores as well.

At the same time, large bookstore chains like Borders and Barnes & Noble, with their buying power and pricing control over publishers, took market share away from small independent bookstores. Big Box retailers returned the favor and used

their even greater buying power to discount popular titles still further, impacting Borders and Barnes & Noble.

Later, the internet came into being as a publicly available

medium in 1993. With all of its stops and starts, and successes and failures (think of the dot-com boom and bust), the internet has now fully come into force as the primary medium of information exchange, socialization and commerce for the grandchildren of those early mall shoppers from the 1950s.

While the internet was growing in popularity, Jeff Bezos, a bright Wall Street banker who had been analyzing the growth potential of e-commerce, was quick to understand the potential of this new channel. In 1994, Jeff and his wife drove across the country in his Dad's car to begin selling books on the internet out of a rented house in Seattle.

The Age of Amazon had begun…

Disruption, reinvention and the overturning of established retail models and businesses are nothing new. It's a story that plays out time and again throughout history. Human invention and the technologies we have developed have constantly demanded re-imagining commerce and retail. This has resulted in a seemingly never-ending stream of changes, from the invention of agriculture and the development of cities, to seafaring ships resulting in trade, to the development of materials and larger buildings to house commerce.

The constantly expanding range of merchandise that trade and then science have made possible made consumer shopping the constantly evolving phenomenon that it is today. But the scale and speed of change we're experiencing now? That really *is* different.

So that's how we got here. But where *are* we?

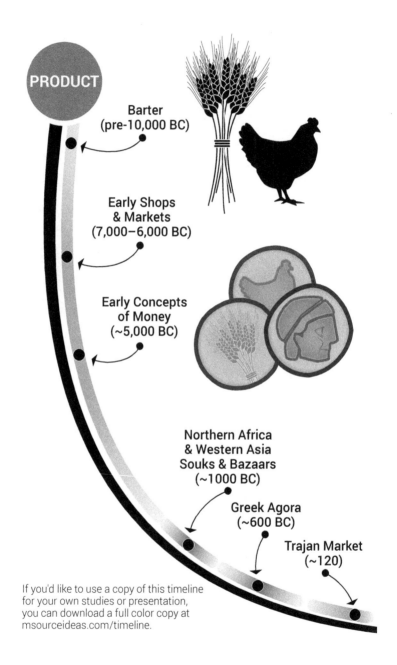

PRODUCT

Barter
(pre-10,000 BC)

Early Shops
& Markets
(7,000–6,000 BC)

Early Concepts
of Money
(~5,000 BC)

Northern Africa
& Western Asia
Souks & Bazaars
(~1000 BC)

Greek Agora
(~600 BC)

Trajan Market
(~120)

If you'd like to use a copy of this timeline
for your own studies or presentation,
you can download a full color copy at
msourceideas.com/timeline.

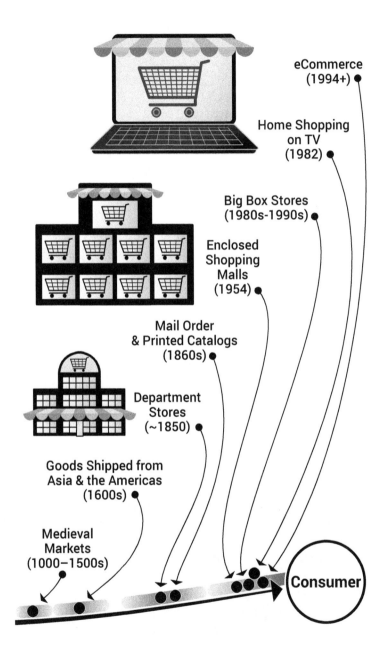

Part II. The Present

Chapter 2.

The Disruption

Now we're ready to take a close look at the state of the current disruptions in retail. We've reviewed the history of retail development: fundamental changes, like the development of agriculture and money, as well as the displacement of downtowns by shopping malls and chain bookstores disrupting locally-owned ones. It's a cycle that has always existed and will likely continue as far into the future as we can imagine.

The disruption (from the Latin *disruptus,* "to break") that e-commerce, enabled by the internet, is having on retail ranks right up there with the enormity of the change. It is possibly even as momentous as the development of agriculture or the introduction of money. But while those changes developed over thousands of years, the speed of the change of e-commerce in the present era is astounding.

In Chapter 4, we'll look at some of the results of this disruption as evidenced by the current state of the industry. But for now, let's look at exactly how the internet and online shopping have affected physical stores and product accessibility.

Yes, we know that e-commerce is growing and will continue to grow at the expense of legacy physical stores but let's explore this further. It's important to our story to get a bit theoretical and examine the fundamental causes of the disruption.

Places

Let's start by looking at the concept of places or even just the concept of "place." What does "place" refer to? My thesaurus tells me it could mean anything from: "to locate" (a verb), to nouns like a "space" or even a "home." (My place or yours?)

Marketers have been practicing marketing ever since early traders haggled millennia ago in the Agora of Rome and the souks of Marrakesh, Morocco, as we saw in Chapter 1.

Marketing theory has only recently been developed in the 20th century. Classic marketing theory talks about a marketing mix of four factors—the four "Ps" found in most marketing text books: **P**roduct, **P**rice, **P**lace and **P**romotion.[6]

It is this concept of *place* as a key aspect of marketing a product that we will delve into further here. In this sense, place means availability. It is the aspect of marketing a product that has to do with how a consumer researches, discovers and acquires the item, as well as how it is delivered to them. In other words, how it's distributed.

As mentioned in the introduction, it is this element of marketing that I've spent my career working with and teasing out. And it is this place or availability marketing aspect that e-commerce disrupts in the most fundamental ways.

The ease of use, trustworthiness and effectiveness of search engines (Google, and now Amazon, for products) means that finding the "right" thing or solution online is astonishingly easy. The friction of finding information about products has been virtually eliminated, and the trust that online consumer reviews provide makes it easier for potential buyers to make a confident decision.

Before the internet, information about what was available involved visiting your local store or mall so you could talk to informed sales staff. And there were always catalogs and recommendations from your friends and neighbors as well as publications like *Consumer Reports*. But the time and effort it took to research a new product or service could be considerable.

The Internet Has Exploded Place

Availability, then, applies to *information* about products, not just the products themselves. It is the abundance of free, frictionless product information that the internet, further facilitated by smartphones, has made possible. Products no longer need to be near consumers in stores, assuming that shipping speed and cost are similar. If product information is freely available online, then product proximity to the consumer matters less.

To state this more succinctly, when information is local, the product doesn't need to be. This is the fundamental reason for the disruption the internet has caused to traditional retail.

In the next chapter, we'll take a closer look at which products still "want" to be close to consumers and why—products like food. And we'll look at which categories of products no longer need to be proximate to their consumers. But as we'll see, surprisingly in many cases and for different reasons, they still will be.

.

Distribution Channels

Let's look at the concept of distribution channels, which are the infrastructure of how a product gets from its producer all the way to its final destination, where it is consumed or used. Distribution channels have always been a fundamental aspect of how products have been made available to consumers. Interestingly, the Latin root of the word "channel" is *canalis*, meaning "canal." It's an apt metaphor for how products flow down a distribution channel from their source through various stages and businesses to the consumer.

The purpose of a distribution channel was, and is, to move a range of products into physical proximity to us, the consumer. Manufacturers, growers, distributors and retailers collaborate to move a reasonable selection of products to within reach at our local store.

Did you ever wonder how the apple you bought at the grocery store got there? That apple metaphorically flowed down through a distribution channel from a tree in, say, Wakima Valley, Washington, to your grocery store through these steps.

A Simplified Distribution Channel

That distribution channel consists of intermediaries (middlemen), wholesalers and retailers. Depending on the type of product, there may be many more steps between the producer of the product and the consumer.

Our Washington apple was probably bought from the grower by a local buying co-operative that consolidates apples from multiple growers. It then went through another stage or two perhaps before reaching a wholesaler, then a distributor, and finally the shelf in your local grocery store. These so-called middlemen play a significant role in performing economic functions.

The local buying co-operative amasses enough apples from several farms for the wholesaler. And the wholesalers and distributors store and transport the apples around the country to retailers. Distributors turn truckloads into pallets, breaking down large quantities into smaller amounts a store can handle. Then the retailer breaks a pallet of apples down into the quantity you as a consumer might want, say a pound's worth or even just a single apple.

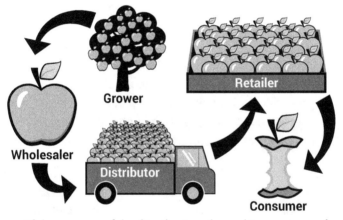

If the purpose of the distribution channel is to get a product from its source to the store, what is the purpose of a store?

Retail Stores

The very name "store" captures that most basic function of retail: to store items within reach of consumers; to make them available. To go back to our four Ps of marketing, that's the Place aspect: making something accessible and available in the right quantity—a bag of apples, a can of soup or a laptop computer.

As we will explore later, the developing function of a retailer in the future will be to provide experience, discovery and education about products. So perhaps we should change the name of what we now call a "store" to the "experience"—but more on this later.

The compelling economic logic of online retail is that it eliminates the need for local stores to carry inventory. To the extent that consumers prefer to order products online, the traditional distribution channels we've described, at least the more downstream parts of them, become less necessary.

Let's Get Theoretical—
Theories, Models and Heuristics

A heuristic is any approach to problem-solving, learning or discovery that employs a practical method not guaranteed to be optimal or perfect, but sufficient for the immediate goals.

Wikipedia

If traditional distribution channels, supply chains and the need for products to be stored locally are being disrupted, what will this do to places, such as the towns and communities we live in?

The academic discipline of economic geography can help us look more closely at this. Central Place Theory (or "CPT") is a model that explains the relationships between goods and services, of which retail stores are a significant part, and the make-up, size and distribution of cities, towns and villages around a country or region.[7] This theory was developed by Walter Christaller, a German geographer, who asserted that settlements simply functioned as "central places" providing services to surrounding areas.[8]

Large cities require, and can therefore make viable, a large variety of consumer and business goods and services. Smaller towns require, and can therefore only support, a smaller variety of products and services.

A second, complementary model that further explains this is W.J. Reilly's "Law of retail gravitation."[9] According to Reilly's model, customers are willing to travel longer distances to larger retail centers because they offer a larger selection of goods and services. The benefit the greater selection of goods and services a larger city offers outweighs the inconvenience and cost of traveling there.

Reilly's model uses the analogy of gravity, in which objects of greater density exert a stronger pull than those that are less dense. Like gravity, larger towns have a greater power to attract or pull consumers because they have a larger selection of goods and services. Essentially, they have a stronger retail gravity.

Take fashion apparel and accessories... A large city will have many types of department and specialty stores offering a copious variety of clothes and accessories for men, women and children. It will have high fashion, teen fashions, menswear, shoes and accessories of all kinds. And that larger selection offered by a city will draw shoppers from long distances.

Obviously, a smaller town will have far fewer clothing stores, and those stores will sell only a relatively small selection of clothing styles and sizes chosen specifically because they will sell well to that comparatively smaller and more local community.

To illustrate this concept of retail gravitation, I'll share an experience I had in early December one year. I had a business meeting in Minneapolis. The hotel I was staying at happened to be near both Minneapolis airport and the Mall of America, the largest shopping mall in the U.S. The hotel shuttle bus and the hotel I was staying at were packed with families shopping for the upcoming holiday season at the Mall of America. I got into a conversation with some of them in the hotel lobby and I was amazed to learn that many of them had driven hundreds of miles to come there to shop, some from as far away as Iowa and even Chicago, Illinois.

This is the perfect of example of Reilly's law of retail gravitation. A large variety of retail goods and services exerts a very strong gravitational attraction. The pull of the selection outweighs the time and travel friction and costs that consumers expend to get there.

CPT explains that, all things being equal, like the quality of roads and the intervening terrain, large cities will be relatively equally spaced around a nation. Towns will be more numerous than cities and spaced farther apart in a uniform pattern of hexagonal areas that form the "market area" around a town. And smaller villages will also be spaced farther apart but distributed in a uniform way.

Together, Christaller's Central Place Theory and Reilly's Law of Retail Gravitation provide ways to understand, especially pre-internet, the relationships between the size and placement of communities, the goods and services that are available, and how shoppers weigh factors like travel costs against availability of products.

The internet has loosened those relationships and will continue to do so. How exactly has yet to be determined. I'm sure that these theories are being re-calibrated and new ones will be developed to explain and predict how concepts like retail gravitation have been influenced by e-commerce.

But what we can say is that, from a strictly fulfillment perspective, if a product doesn't need to be stored locally because you can order it online, then that product doesn't "need" to be stored in a retail shop locally. And yes, this may affect the characteristics, sizes and spacing of towns that at least partly existed to provide services, including retail stores, to their market areas.

In smaller rural communities, routine goods, such as groceries and basic clothing, that can be easily discovered, researched and ordered online will likely become increasingly less available in local brick-and-mortar stores.

The relationships between online and offline availability of consumer products and the sometimes surprising linkages between them have been studied by Wharton School of Business Professor David Bell and are explained in some detail in his excellent book *Location is Still Everything*.

But as we will see later in this book, the fulfillment aspect of retail is not the only consideration. There are facets of retail that cannot be fully replaced by online commerce, and many types of retail that involve much more than simply making a product available. One such crucial retail component is *discovery*.

In the next chapter, we are going to take a more detailed look at what types of products and shopping occasions are most suitable to online shopping, and which are more likely to "want" to be purchased or at least discovered and researched in physical stores, as well as why.

Chapter 3.

How We Shop

All models are wrong, but some are useful.[10]

George Box

The quotation above provides a suitable frame of reference for this chapter. All models have their limits, but there's value in some of them as well. With that in mind, we're going to take a closer look at how shoppers buy products.

We'll reference some ideas from classic marketing theory as we did earlier when we looked at the concept of Place in the four Ps of marketing. We're also going to bring some of these ideas together into a new heuristic to try to understand the types of shopping that are more and less likely to gravitate farther online, and why.

Two Fundamental Aspects of the Buyer's Journey

There are many theories about how consumers shop and the

different stages they go through on the way to a purchase—from awareness of a need, to researching and considering options, to deciding what to buy and where to buy it from. These stages are known as the "buyer's journey."

For now, we're going to radically simplify things with respect to how people use the internet and physical stores to shop. We're going to start by saying that there are two fundamental aspects to shopping—discovery and fulfillment.

Discovery covers all the aspects of finding out about a product, researching the best fit for our needs, the best place to buy it, and the best price.

Fulfillment covers the process of purchasing and receiving those products.

Let me start with a couple of examples to illustrate. A college student sits in her bedroom in her parents' home in the New York suburbs shopping for a new computer. She's browsing the internet on her old, slow laptop with a cracked screen. Soon she will be driving through leafy hills to the upstate college she attends. It's her junior year. If she's already decided on a Dell and doesn't need any advice on the model, she can buy it directly from Dell's website (fulfillment).

That would be cutting out the retailer and the usual distribution channels. In this case, there is no fundamental discovery process. She has already decided on what brand to buy, Dell, and where to buy it, the Dell website.

In this instance, discovery only involves deciding what product specifications she needs—8MG or 12MG of ram, 14″ or 15.6″ screen, etc. And in this case, buying it on the Dell website makes the most sense. It is the most efficient way to fulfill that retail purchase.

However, if our student is just starting out on her buyer

journey, and is still deciding on a make and model, she is in discovery mode. She might visit a Best Buy store to see a full range of brands and maybe get some advice. In this case, Best Buy, the brick–and-mortar retailer, offers the valuable service of making a wide variety of brands and products available, and helping her with the discovery process.

Best Buy's role in this process is to make a range of brands, products and information available (through literature and perhaps consumer reviews printed out on the store shelf or certainly available online) and to provide knowledgeable sales staff who help the consumer discover and decide what is the best fit for them. In this way, the consumer can discover the best solution for their needs.

After having checked out HP, Microsoft, Acer and Lenovo models in the store, maybe our student would still end up buying that Dell, either from Best Buy or directly from Dell's website, but you can see the value of what the retailer does. They provide local availability of a range of products, as well as information and service, but the fundamental function of the store is discovery. The fulfillment aspect may or may not be carried out by the store. The store doesn't need to stock a large inventory of every item they carry if they have an effective e-commerce site. They can stock larger quantities of popular items, while displaying many "long-tail" items (products with lower demand) for customers to learn about and experience in the store, but which don't need to be carried locally since they can be ordered online.

Understanding the difference between discovery and fulfillment helps us to grasp how the different properties of both online and offline shopping can contribute to an ideal consumer shopping experience.

Some aspects of discovery, such as accessing product technical specifications, user reviews and pricing are best carried out online. Other facets of discovery are related to the senses, such as trying on clothes for their fit, seeing fabric colors, and feeling textures. Therefore, they must be carried out in a store or by ordering products online to be delivered to us just to evaluate them and returned if they don't meet our needs.

As for product fulfillment, online ordering with home delivery is the better option for routine items and when we can wait for delivery. At other times, while we are in the store for another reason or because we need the product immediately, in-store pick-up will be preferable.

So, there we have it—two aspects of a shopper's retail journey: discovery and fulfillment.

With this simplified model in mind, let's take a closer look at the types of products and shopping occasions that are more suitable to take place online, offline or, more often, in combination.

First, we'll look at two marketing frameworks related to consumer products.

Classic Marketing Framework

In academic marketing theory, consumer products are divided up into four product classes having to do with the characteristics of the products and the way they are purchased. These are: convenience, shopping, specialty and unsought products.[11]

Convenience Products

These are lower cost, routinely purchased products. Consumers usually don't invest much time or mental effort to evaluate these purchases. Examples include household staples, like cereal, bread, laundry detergent and toothpaste.

A sub-category of convenience products is emergency products, like an umbrella when it's raining.

Shopping Products

These are products that consumers want to invest time, thought and energy for researching and comparing competing brands.

In classic marketing theory, shopping products are further divided into homogeneous and heterogeneous products.

Homogeneous means the same—interchangeable. For example, any 8GB laptop with an Intel i7 processor and full HD display will be functionally the same across different brands, like Dell, HP or Lenovo. 8,000 BTU air conditioners will all cool a 300-square foot room, regardless of the brand. Product attributes, brand and, of course, price are the key factors.

Heterogeneous products are different from one another. They are unique and therefore less substitutable. Furniture is an example. Different types of sofas have many functional and more subtle nuances between them—size, leather or fabric, softness, texture and color. Another example is clothing. Even basic items like t-shirts have many differences—size, structure, fabric content, weight and texture.

Fresh meat and produce provide another example. The different cuts of meat and the zucchini and tomatoes at the market are not all the same. At least for some people, comparing and picking them out is half the fun. We'll investigate this more fully later in this chapter.

For heterogeneous products:

Often the consumer expects help from a knowledgeable salesperson. Quality and style matter more than price. In

> fact, once the customer finds the right product, price may not matter if it's reasonable... Branding may be less important for heterogeneous shopping products. The more carefully consumers compare price and quality, the less they rely on brand names or labels.[12]

Heterogeneous products often must be compared in person, like the experience products found in the Search and Experience Framework, on the following page.

Specialty Products

These are products a consumer really wants and will seek out, such as a brand. For example, Apple products or the Swiss watch brand Patek Philippe. Any brand that consumers aren't willing to accept substitutes for are specialty products.

Unsought Products

These are products that consumers don't search for. There are two types of unsought products, new and regular.

New unsought products are often newly introduced products. An example would be the Fitbit activity trackers a few years ago. These were unsought because, as new products, consumers didn't know they existed. As shoppers learned about them, they became shopping or specialty products.

Regular unsought products are products (or services) that have been in existence but are not generally sought out. Examples might include non-profits, such as the American Red Cross, or funeral services. Consumers may be aware they exist but aren't that motivated to research them.

OK, that's one marketing framework for sorting out different product and shopping types. Let's move on to another framework.

Search and Experience Framework

Marketing academics have also divided products into three further types that are worth taking a brief look at. These are search goods, experience goods and credence goods.[13]

Search goods are products that you pretty much know what you're going to get ahead of time, either because you've bought it before (like those California rolls from the local sushi place) or because the item has predictable characteristics, like AA batteries. These types of goods lend themselves well to being researched online for availability and price, and often don't need to be experienced in person before purchasing.

Experience goods are products whose value can be assessed more by experiencing them in person and perhaps consuming them, like men's suits or a bottle of wine. It's hard to evaluate these products ahead of time or online. Of course, if you trust other consumers' online reviews, you don't need to experience them before buying—you can rely on other people's experience.

Finally, *credence goods* are products, or more likely, services, where you may not know if they have worked correctly even after you've purchased and used them. This could be something like home heating system tune-ups or surgery.

Combining Frameworks

Keeping in mind the limitations and usefulness of conceptual models, we'll now combine aspects of the two marketing frameworks just discussed into one new two-axis model.

This will be useful for analyzing consumer products and shopping occasions, as well as for plotting the types of products and shopping mostly likely to move further online and conversely which types of products are most likely to remain offline. Most importantly, this two-axis framework will help us understand why.

Two-Axis Model Framework

Axis 1: From Homogeneous to Heterogeneous Products

In the first framework we went over earlier, there were four classes of products; convenience, shopping, specialty and unsought. Then shopping products were further divided into homogeneous and heterogeneous.

Our first axis builds on these two ways of looking at products. Since homogeneous means "sameness," in our analysis, these products are relatively indistinguishable from one another. They are machine-made and mass-produced products for the most part. For example, different brands of laptop computers with 8GB memory, 15.6″ HD screens and Intel i7 processors. While not literally the "same" as each another, they are similar. They are loosely homogeneous and could be substituted for one another.

Homogeneous products, due to their functional sameness and relative interchangeability, are like search goods in the second framework model, above. They can easily be researched online, both by functional attributes and price. They do not require in-person inspection, nor do they need to be experienced in person, especially if online reviews by other consumers confirm the performance of the product. As in the laptop example, an 8GB laptop with an Intel i7 processor can be researched comfortably online.

Heterogeneous products have the opposite qualities of uniqueness. They are either one-of-a-kind, such as an antique or handcrafted product, or other items that are similar but not interchangeable. For example, every hand-finished wooden coffee table of the same model will have slight but important differences in grain and finish, which is part of their appeal.

A plum-colored wool cardigan has many details that are hard to evaluate on a screen with just product descriptions to go on, even when they have consumer reviews as well. To really evaluate the subtleties of color, fabric texture, button construction and, of course, fit, this type of product must be experienced.

To tie this into our second framework (search, experience and credence analysis), heterogeneous products can be loosely interchanged with experience products.

The homogeneous/heterogeneous continuum, illustrated below, analyzes products according to their properties of being the same or unique. In the image below, homogeneous, or sameness, is on the left and heterogeneous, or uniqueness, is on the right.

Axis 2: Customer Engagement

The second set of qualities, situated on our vertical axis, indicates a consumer's level of emotional engagement with a purchase.

At the bottom of the vertical axis are low-engagement products and buying occasions. These are where a product is viewed as merely functional, such as pasta, laundry detergent and paper towels.

In the classic marketing framework analysis, low-engagement products are equivalent to convenience products. They are routine, often-purchased, usually lower cost, household staples.

And at the top of the axis are products and shopping occasions that consumers find more important and rewarding. Examples include shopping for a car, home furnishings or clothing.

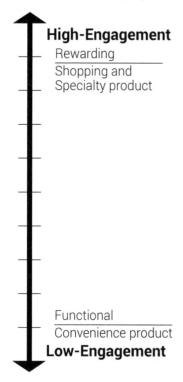

Likely, this high engagement will have a lot to do with the price point of the item, as well as how long the buyer will have to live with the product because of its durability and quality. But not always. Consumers who are home chefs may be highly engaged in buying produce, for example, while others may find this to be more routine.

Drawing the parallel again with our product classes framework, high-engagement shopping occasions would be roughly equivalent with shopping products and specialty products. Again, these are products that consumers care deeply about—products for which they will invest time researching and comparing options. They are often more expensive because they are an expression of their lifestyle. And they include brands that consumers have a strong attachment to, like Apple computers or a Patek Philippe watch. Here is a more detailed image, tying the two axes together.

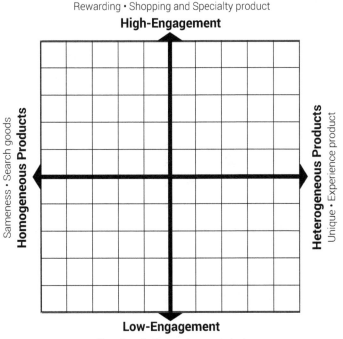

Rewarding • Shopping and Specialty product
High-Engagement

Sameness • Search goods
Homogeneous Products

Heterogeneous Products
Unique • Experience product

Low-Engagement
Functional • Convenience product

Exploring the Quadrants

It's important to understand that mapping products into the two-axis framework is a subjective exercise because so much depends on the consumer's perspective of shopping for a given product. The loyalty a consumer feels toward a specific brand or purchase may take what once was a high-engagement experience and turn it into a low one. However, by understanding the potential perception of consumers, we can predict which buying occasions are likely to require an in-person experience and which may very well move online.

Let's look at some examples. In the illustration that follows, we will move around from the top left quadrant, clockwise.

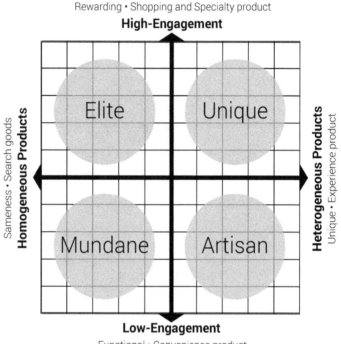

Rewarding • Shopping and Specialty product
High-Engagement

Sameness • Search goods
Homogeneous Products

Elite

Unique

Heterogeneous Products
Unique • Experience product

Mundane

Artisan

Low-Engagement
Functional • Convenience product

Homogeneous and High-Engagement

Products in this first quadrant are homogeneous and high-engagement. We'll call them "Elite" products. These are highly-researched purchases for which shoppers are seeking as near-perfect a solution as possible for their need. And they want an exceptional experience buying them as well. Examples of Elite products include cars, high-end electronics, fine jewelry and accessories, and other high-status items.

This type of purchase is unlikely to move online because the personalized nature of the shopping experience is potentially as essential to the consumer as the product they are buying.

For example, Patek Philippe is probably the most prestigious high-end Swiss watch manufacturer in the world. (Note: I don't own one, unfortunately.) Based in Geneva, the company was founded in 1851. Their retail prices for a watch start at $7,600 and average around $20,000, going up to as much as $1.5M. They have a high resale value and are often passed down from generation to generation as heirlooms.

This product is partially machine-made, although assembled partly by hand. It is homogeneous in that any Patek Philippe watch of the same model and production year will be identical to another, except for the grain of the leather band if it has one. It is a high-engagement shopping occasion because, as an expensive, heirloom-quality piece of jewelry, a buyer will be emotionally engaged in its purchase.

This kind of purchase, while it is likely to be researched online, is unlikely actually to be made online (although they are available), because the shopper will value a high-touch, personal purchasing experience. They may seek personal advice on their selection from a well-informed salesperson in a store, who can explain in detail the differences between the various models and features.

The same type of purchasing dynamics apply to other items that share the same qualities, from cars to fine jewelry to expensive computers and other home electronics.

Heterogeneous and High-Engagement

Next, in the top right quadrant of the two-axis model, are heterogeneous, high-engagement purchases. We'll call these

"Unique" products. These are products and buying occasions where the consumer wants a richly rewarding, memorable experience, because they are buying items that are highly important to them and are expressions of themselves.

When a consumer is shopping for items in this quadrant, it's not so much about the experience of shopping as it is about the opportunity to buy something unusual and personally desirable.

We'll use the example of buying a cherished piece of antique or hand-made furniture. It is a high-engagement shopping opportunity for a unique product. The emotional reason for buying (vertical axis)—self-expression, aesthetics, even financial investment—combined with the need to evaluate, see and touch the qualities of such an experiential product (horizontal axis) make these types of occasions unlikely to move online at scale.

Of course, researching antiques or crafts dealers and learning about different historical periods of furniture, as well as materials and production methods, would be suitable to carry out online. However, this research likely would be supplemented by an in-person interaction with a knowledgeable antique or crafts dealer.

Other products in this category include many higher-end clothing purchases, home furnishings and the like.

Heterogeneous and Low-Engagement

In the lower right quadrant of the two-axis model, you'll find heterogeneous lower-engagement products called "Artisan" products. These have qualities of uniqueness, but are lower on the engagement scale.

Examples range from produce, fresh-prepared and artisanal foods at the grocery store to personal care products, cosmetics and home accessories. These are items that are lower in engagement, but still provide a pleasant shopping occasion and reward to buy, even if they are routinely purchased.

Some of these items are moving online, but will likely often be purchased in physical stores due to their uniqueness and experiential qualities.

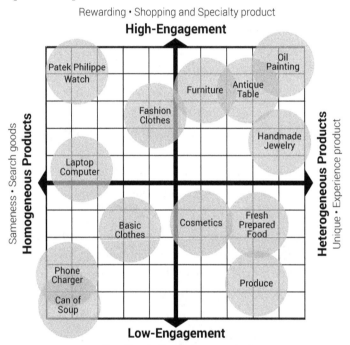

In the case of fresh and prepared foods, to the extent these types of products can be delivered quickly and at high enough quality levels, these are moving online. Amazon's purchase of Whole Foods Market shows the potential for this.

The next chapter, "The Current State of Retail," explores how all large grocery retailers are scrambling to implement home-delivery services of both shelf-stable and fresh food. Home delivery of restaurant foods is also becoming increasingly viable and ubiquitous due to ordering platforms like Grubhub.

Homogeneous and Low-Engagement

Finally, in the lower left quadrant of the two-axis model, you will find homogeneous, lower-engagement purchases. We'll call them "Mundane."

These are the functional, mass-produced and reliable staples of everyday life. This category of products and buying occasions are most suitable to online shopping since it alleviates the consumer's perceived chore of shopping for them.

There are countless examples of Mundane products, including:

- household items, like paper towels and detergent.
- shelf-stable packaged foods, like cereal and pasta.
- basic clothing, like sports socks.
- numerous other durable, technical, lower-cost functional purchases that have already moved online for the most part, like phone chargers.

Product sameness (in other words, the absence of a need to see and touch the item) and consumers' relative low-engagement with these low-impact purchases are the common features of these routine purchases. However, factors like the cost of shipping bulk items and the speed of delivery will affect when these items will be purchased online. If we're out of pasta, and a spaghetti dinner is on the home menu, we're probably not waiting around for the UPS guy or other delivery service.

Personal items, for example, socks, are also prime candidates for future replacement and replenishment by online purchase methods, once we've experienced them for fit as well as fabric weight, texture and color.

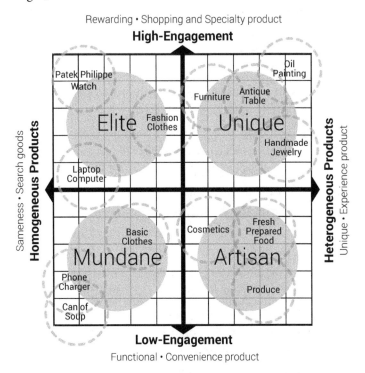

Rewarding • Shopping and Specialty product

When the Buying Experience Itself is Heterogeneous

A couple more examples I want to look at are more situation-specific purchases. These are circumstances where the actual process of buying the product and the uniqueness of the purchase are fixed in a time and place. For example, the "treasure hunt" of a shopping experience at a discounter like T.J. Maxx and buying a souvenir.

On our two-axis chart, these would be plotted at the top, but in the middle. That is because they are high-engagement purchasing situations, but the products themselves might have been purchased online. You could have found that shirt you bought at T.J. Maxx somewhere else, either offline or online. But the reward of getting a deal on something perfect that you found unexpectedly stimulates the spontaneous purchase.

Recently I bought some coffee mugs from a Minnesota-themed gift shop in the Minneapolis airport. The experience of buying them from a knowledgeable salesperson with whom I had chatted about the local economy and Minneapolis' arts culture stays with me when I use those mugs in our home. It was the uniqueness of the experience and situation that prompted the purchase, and of course could never have meaningfully been replaced by an online purchase.

With an understanding of the two-axis model now in place, we'll proceed to look at the current state of online and offline retail, as well as related areas like shopping malls. We'll also examine how different retail models are likely to develop in the foreseeable future based on the predictions we can infer from the shopping preferences of buyers.

Chapter 4.

The Current State of Retail

Having taken a close look at how the emergence of online retail has disrupted traditional supply chains and shopping in Chapter 2, and at models of shopping behavior in Chapter 3, let's look at the results of the current disruptions in the U.S. retail environment.

We'll take a brief survey of the current state of online sales, retail stores, malls, food retail, restaurants and consumer brands. The events and trends described here are already in the process of happening as this book is being written. Some of these changes are still in the beginning stages, while others are further along.

Some Facts

These facts apply to the U.S. economy in early 2018, but it's safe to say that they're generally representative of other developed economies in the world.

- Of the $5.07 trillion spent in the U.S. retail economy in 2017, approximately 13% of those transactions were conducted online.[14]

- Online sales are growing faster than offline sales.
- 2017 total retail sales grew 4.2% over 2016.[15]
- 2017 online sales grew 16% over 2016.

Clearly total retail sales are growing, but the online component of those sales is a significant part of that growth—around 40%. And Amazon represents almost half of those online sales.

It's estimated that online sales will reach 17% of all retail by 2022.[16]

Yet it's important to remember that a significant part of those online sales are the e-commerce sales of omni-channel retailers like Macy's, Walmart and Target.

Over-Stored

America has an abundance of retail space. Billions of bricks and tons of mortar make up the 23.6 square feet of retail space per person in the U.S., according to an article in *Fast Company* "The Future of Retail in the Age of Amazon."[17] Is that a lot? Yep! Compare that with Australia at 11.1 square feet and the U.K. at 4.6 per capita. Overall, Europe only has 2.5 square feet of retail space per person.[18]

Retail expert Robin Lewis further writes in the same article:

Since 1995, the number of shopping centers in the U.S. has grown by more than 23% and GLA (total gross leasable area) by almost 30%, while the population has grown by less than 14%.[19]

Why so much retail space in the U.S.? Capital was cheap and available, and imported goods were becoming ever-cheaper due to the developing economies of countries like China and India.

For retailers and their investors, there has been both the motive and the opportunity to simply build more stores.

Opening retail stores that are essentially unnecessary has been a key part of retailers' competitive strategy. Anything to bump up sales.

The above statistics are for the overall retail market. If we break out food retail separately, the changes are even more dramatic. Of the roughly 24 square feet per capita of retail space in the U.S., 4 square feet of that is food retail. The amount of retail space in the U.S. allocated to food retail has increased 30 times since 1950.[20]

In 2017, almost 7,000 retail stores closed in the U.S.[21] By contrast, in 2016 only 1,674 stores closed.[22]

As is so often the case, these facts and figures don't tell the whole story because the net number of retail stores in the U.S. is still increasing. Store closings were heavily weighted toward a few chains such as Radio Shack and Payless ShoeSource.

The number of stores in the U.S. actually grew by 4,000 stores in 2017. So yes, some companies are closing stores, but overall more stores are being opened than closed.[23]

New store openings in 2018 are heavily concentrated in the discount, grocery and convenience store sectors. Lidl, a German food discounter like Aldi who already has a strong U.S. presence, is just now entering the U.S. market. Lidl is planning on opening 100 stores in the U.S. in the next two years and up to 600 thereafter. Aldi is opening 200 new stores as well. Walmart and Kroger, a grocery retailer, both plan to open at least 50 stores each in the next year. And Dollar General, Dollar Tree and 7-Eleven are all opening hundreds of new stores.

While it seems there may be "too many" retail stores in the U.S., until retail businesses and their investors stop vying for market share, the number of physical stores in the U.S. is unlikely to recede quickly. Which is, of course, unlikely to happen, especially in the food and drug industries where competition is so strong. After all, securing a "bigger piece of the pie" is how they stay in business.

The cost of opening each individual store is relatively inexpensive, so retailers open far more stores than are "needed" to build their brand in the minds of consumers and poach their competition.

In the town where I live, the drugstore chains CVS and Walgreens both opened what are arguably unnecessary stores in our neighborhood. Both are competing with one another for our awareness and brand loyalties for the same purchases.

However, no one doubts that because of the continued growth of e-commerce, retail is being shaken up and reinvented dramatically. Stores only remain viable in certain categories—those categories least vulnerable to online shopping.

What about Malls?

As the fortunes of stores shift, with some chains in retreat, others expanding, and several doing a bit of both, what is clearer is the impact this is having on large enclosed shopping malls.

In the U.S., since 2010 more than two dozen enclosed shopping malls have been closed, and an additional 60 are on the brink according to Green Street Advisors, which tracks the mall industry.[24]

Of the 1,200 malls in the U.S., perhaps 15% are 30-50% vacant.[25]

It seems clear that the move to online shopping is, with increasing speed, going to shutter or at least dramatically change the tenant mixes of many shopping centers.

However, as with our look at retail stores, it is too simplistic to say that the mall itself as a retail phenomenon is in decline. It is closer to the truth to say that the mall industry is and will further become bifurcated—split into higher-end, highly viable malls and the lower strata of malls that will either reinvent themselves with a broader selection of uses or simply die and be re-purposed.

New York University marketing professor Scott Galloway, in his book *The Four* about the dominance of the four tech giants Amazon, Apple, Google and Facebook, writes:

> Forty-four percent of total U.S. mall value, based on sales, size and quality among other measures, now resides with the top hundred properties, out of about a thousand malls.[26]

So the top roughly 10% of malls are doing very well and attracting both tenants and customers.

Going back to our analysis in Chapter 2, these highly successful malls will continue to exert retail gravitational force to attract customers and tenants from their surrounding areas. Some of the more middle-of-the-road malls may remain viable if they imaginatively re-invent their uses to accommodate the lower retail gravitational pull they exert on their market areas.

From our brief history of retail in Chapter 1, we learned that drab, undifferentiated malls that do not provide what the founder of the original department store, Aristide Boucicaut, called "a cathedral of commerce" will not survive. Malls and shopping experiences that do not provide the sense of spectacle and adventure Boucicaut described will not remain viable on any level. Many categories of functional shopping will be replaced by the internet.

Using the terminology of my two-axis model, the types of stores and malls that will continue to have a strong purpose in the future will be those that cater to the Elite and Unique quadrants, and that can leverage the Artisan quadrant to their advantage.

Products in the Elite and Unique quadrants are goods that shoppers are emotionally invested in, and for which they want to have a rich and personal buying experience. The process of buying these products is closely intertwined with the consumer's shopping experience and future enjoyment of their purchase.

Any retailers who sell Artisan products, such as fresh food, will need to leverage the pleasurable and entertaining aspects of shopping to attract consumers. By doing so, they may entice some of these shoppers to buy products from the Mundane quadrant on the same purchasing trip.

Offline retail in all categories will need to use experiences that cannot be replicated online to remain relevant. We'll discuss this in more detail in Chapter 5, where we predict future developments.

Food Retail is Changing

As mentioned in the previous section, the number of grocery stores in the U.S. is still increasing overall. New retail formats like deep discounter Lidl, a longstanding market leader in Germany, are entering the U.S. market. Like the rest of retail, many industry participants would agree that the grocery industry is over-stored. Essentially, too many square feet of grocery store retail space in the U.S. are chasing too few consumers.

The Merging of Restaurant and Grocery

Grocery and prepared food retailing are merging, especially in urban and upscale markets.

The continuum of buying food starts at one end with consumers purchasing raw, unprocessed ingredients for meal preparation, such as produce, meats, seafood and baking staples. This is followed by more processed or partially prepared ingredients like canned soup, deli meats and bread. The far end of this continuum is ready-to-eat items including fresh-made sandwiches, hot prepared food, and salad bars.

If the store provides a seating area, like Whole Foods Market, you might even eat it right there in the store. More likely, you would take it back to your workplace for lunch or home for dinner.

The main dichotomy for grocery is that consumers can purchase ingredients to make food later or they can buy prepared food to eat right away with no preparation other than possibly to heat it up.

As a result, grocery stores and restaurants are becoming more similar and playing on one another's turf.

Center Aisle Grocery Products Are in Transition

Different types of food within the grocery store raise questions related to the theme of our book. Most importantly, what components of a grocery store's inventory are likely to be purchased online for delivery?

Going back to our analysis of what a store does, we must ask: In an electronic-ordering age, to what extent does food inventory need to be stored locally?

Shelf-stable, non-perishable grocery items like canned and packaged food and paper products are what grocery retailers call "center-aisle products." This is because they are found on the shelving in the center areas of most grocery stores.

These are most amenable to being ordered online and delivered with no detrimental impact to quality because they're shelf-stable and indestructible, can be left on your doorstep, and are not that expensive. And if you've had an Amazon Key installed as your front door lock, your Amazon courier can even leave them inside your house. Next stop? Your refrigerator! But I'm getting ahead of myself… We'll get into more detail on what the future of fresh food delivery will look like in Chapter 5, "The Future."

The fresher the food product or the less processed it is, the less suitable these items are for online ordering and delivery. The only exception is when online ordering leads to immediate delivery, such as a restaurant delivery.

Grocery Retailers and the Problem of Fresh Home-Delivered Food

Grocery retailers have been attempting to achieve profitable home-delivery of fresh food in an industry with an already very slim profit margin.

Most grocery store chains are experimenting with this, including Whole Foods Market (now Amazon), Walmart, Kroger, Costco, and many others—and not only with the easier-to-deliver center-aisle non-perishable items mentioned earlier. In some markets, they are also delivering perishable items like dairy, meat and produce. Clearly these services can only be provided profitably in the most densely populated areas of the country. And even in those areas, achieving profitable home-delivery of food is a challenge.

There are several models of grocery store home delivery. Third-party companies like Instacart and Shipt (recently acquired by Target stores)[27] offer an online platform for consumers to order from. These companies then use a network of independent shoppers to pick products from brick-and-mortar grocery store shelves to deliver to consumers.

Some grocery retailers like Walmart and Kroger are testing grocery home delivery services through partnerships with the ride-sharing companies Uber and Lyft.

There are also businesses, such as NetGrocer and Peapod, that operate warehouses of grocery products and use their own delivery services with their own employees.

Restaurants Are Doubling as Production Kitchens

Restaurants are increasingly offering home delivery services, which brings us back to Jim Cramer and his quote from the opening of this book.

Cramer, on business cable TV channel CNBC, said in early 2017:

> Younger consumers don't want to go out, they just want to order food on Grubhub, so they can stay on their couch and keep playing "Call of Duty."

It's true. People are staying in more and ordering food online. Many restaurants, from fine dining establishments to Panera Bread to McDonald's, are using online ordering apps to allow customers to order online and have their food delivered. This is true for eating at home, but also for lunch at work. Increasingly, workers don't want to spend time away from the office to go out to eat. Restaurants are also increasingly offering the option of ordering online and having their meal ready to pick up, rather than waiting at the restaurant.

The food ordering app Grubhub, along with their several subsidiaries Seamless, DiningIn, Delivered Dish and others, deliver food to consumer's homes and workplaces from 55,000 restaurants in 1,200 cities in the U.S. and the U.K. Their app allows for a frictionless experience, offering a range of food options available in your zip code along with consumer reviews.

As we noted in Chapter 2, the restaurant business model is changing due to the availability of high quality online information aggregated in one place about what ready-to-eat food is available in your neighborhood, along with pricing and reviews. As ordering online and delivery services become increasingly widespread, to some degree, restaurants will think of themselves as local commercial food production kitchens as much as restaurants.

Some higher end restaurants have created order-only sub-brands for this purpose. For example, Seaside's (a division of Oyster Bah in Chicago), and Ando (by Momofuku founder David Chang in New York) were created only for delivery service and have no customer dining areas at all.[28]

There are also specialized food companies, known as "virtual restaurants," that operate from commercial kitchens whose entire purpose is to produce ready-to-eat food for home delivery. An example of this model is Green Summit Group in New York City. These food production operations are not open to the public and have no walk-in counter or dining area. They are strategically located in lower rent areas near large populations and the same facility might offer several different food categories.[29]

In this chapter we've examined just a few of the contours of the current retail terrain. These can provide early hints to reveal some of the directions and ways in which omni-channel retail is unfolding. Now we'll peek further into the future and make some predictions about where all of this is headed.

Part III. The Future

Chapter 5.

The Future

I n this final chapter, I'll continue some of the threads from the preceding chapter and examine adjacent areas of omni-channel retail as well. I will also share some informed speculation to make a few predictions about how omni-channel will develop in key areas.

The Future of Retailers and Brands

Retailers have always been brands—Nordstrom, Macy's, Target, The Gap—and they have consistently created private label brands for products, too. Sears created its appliance brand, Kenmore, to sell sewing machines back in 1913 when they were still just a catalog retailer. Fashion brands like Ralph Lauren sell both through other retailers, like Macy's, and through their own branded shops too.

This is equally true of e-commerce. With a 44% share of U.S. online retail, Amazon is unquestionably the leading online retail brand in the minds of many U.S. consumers. They've essentially set consumer expectations for online retail through their huge range of products, consumer reviews and subscription membership program, Prime, which provides free shipping.

The Amazon e-commerce playbook is being rapidly adopted by legacy retailers like Walmart, Target and Kohl's. These companies are well-positioned to compete in omni-channel retail because of their store networks. Having physical stores near much of the U.S. population allows them to fulfill many of their online orders from local inventory. This allows for fast, low-cost shipping to consumers.

In this congested world, product and retailer brands will increasingly jostle to maintain their relevance to consumers. While this jostling is obviously not new, the increasing importance to retail of technology and data will mean that technology companies will merge and partner with consumer brands and retailers in new and unique ways. For example, Google Express, Google's online shopping mall, has already begun to partner with both Walmart and Target to extend their e-commerce reach.

> **My prediction:** We will see many more inventive collaborations between technology and retail companies, going forward.

Private Labels

As we mentioned, Amazon has won the hearts and minds of consumers for many categories and shopping occasions. Increasingly, Amazon is using this lead to offer their own private label versions of products alongside established brands.

AmazonBasics, initially created for categories like phone chargers and batteries, has now expanded to over 1,500 products ranging from luggage to car floor mats and sports equipment.[30] Another brand, Amazon Essentials, is for generic clothing like underwear.

They've also created stylish brands that you wouldn't know are owned by Amazon. For menswear, they've created Goodthreads and Buttoned Down. Ella Moon, Lark & Ro, and Paris Sunday are for women's apparel. Amazon's Scout + Ro brand is for children's clothing. They also have different labels for many other categories from shoes to cosmetics, furniture and tools.

As mentioned earlier, this is not new. Large retailers have always used their reach and traffic to create store brands for their best-selling product categories.

> **My prediction:** Online retailers, using their extensive consumer data, will be able to create private label product brands tailored to consumers and shopping behavior at optimum price points. Market leaders like Nordstrom, Macy's, Kohl's, Target and Walmart will need to do this as well as Amazon to remain competitive.

How Brands and Retailers Are Playing Omni-Channel—Together

Retailer and product brands are co-operating with each other across multiple channels to engage their consumers.

For example, Best Buy, the electronics retailer, uses its physical stores as a showroom for electronics brands like Samsung, LG and Microsoft. These in-store showrooms are staffed by well-trained sales assistants to educate shoppers about their products and are partially paid for by the brands. Best Buy matches its competitors' online prices to discourage store shoppers from buying online elsewhere. This has largely alleviated the consumer's need to check prices.

> The price guarantee made a loyal shopper out of Anton Robinson, a 34-year-old lawyer in New York City. He buys his music equipment from Best Buy because he prefers to test products in person and doesn't have to compare prices. "I want to know what a speaker sounds like. And I know the price point is going to be there."[31]

Since 70% of U.S. consumers live within 15 minutes of a Best Buy store, they are often able to use their stores as warehouses to ship products that have been ordered online. About half of its online orders are either picked up in a store or shipped to the customer from a store.

UPPAbaby, a manufacturer of baby strollers, helps bring foot traffic to their retail partners' stores. For example, they periodically arrange for in-store technicians to provide stroller tune-ups to consumers. And their brick-and-mortar retail partners receive new product releases first, with only older models being sold through Amazon.[32]

Running gear maker Brooks, owned by Berkshire Hathaway, Inc., works with local retailers to combine the richness of an in-store experience with online efficiency.

> In April (2017), Brooks launched a website that lets stores order products they don't have in stock and then drop-ships them directly to customers' homes. The system reduces the likelihood that a retailer will take the time to fit a customer with the perfect shoe, but then lose the sale to an online competitor.[33]

Rick Wilhelm, Vice President of Sales for Brooks, said, "There's no way local stores can carry all five colors of our best-selling shoes," and the new site gives them "the long tail of the web."

Brooks is one of a growing number of brands that are using a service called Locally, which offers another way for brands and retailers to co-operate.

> ...Locally is a startup that lets shoppers check a brand's website for an item and then find out which stores in their neighborhood have it in stock and reserve it for in-store pick up and, in some cases, local delivery.[34]

Swedish company Thule, a maker of bike racks, cargo containers and luggage, is another example. The brand doesn't sell retail on its website. Instead they use a software product by Kibo that directs the shopper to the nearest store that has that item. They allow the most convenient local merchant to the shopper to make the sale, putting the consumer at the center of the equation, much like Uber provides the nearest available ride to the user.[35]

Sports apparel maker Arc'teryx supports its brick-and-mortar resellers by using demographic and location data from its online sales to help its retail partners carry the right products to match the demographics for their location.[36]

What we're seeing here are examples of the many new ways that products can be placed in front of consumers, combining the best aspects of e-commerce with the irreplaceable qualities of physical stores—the essence of omni-channel retail.

My Prediction: The future of retail and the way consumers and brands interact will often span across multiple channels, both electronic and physical. Elite

> brands especially, from the top-left quadrant of our two-axis model, which benefit from a rich, in-store purchasing experience, will increasingly develop new ways to interact with consumers across channels.

Brands Need Online and Offline Presence

Brands are realizing that it is challenging to build a large business with an online-only strategy.

> "It's very hard to launch a brand these days that's just online-only. It's an incredibly difficult and crowded e-commerce environment," said Sucharita Mulpuru, a retail analyst at Forrester Research. She noted there are more than 800,000 online stores, all vying to attract customers through the gateway of Google... "Online real estate has become crowded and expensive. Bidding on keywords against the likes of Amazon and large traditional retailers to land on the first page of search results is a costly game."[37]

In a May 2017 Wall Street Journal article, "Web Retailers Shift Gears," Philip Krim, co-founder of mattress company Casper, revealed his company is in talks with Target to offer the Casper mattresses in stores. In the interview Krim stated, "You have to start with digital...(but) offline distribution—that's where you're really able to get a lot of scale."[38]

Harry's, the shaving products manufacturer, is another brand that started online but is also now being distributed in Target stores. Since being in the stores, Harry's quickly built a 50% share of market for razor handles in Target. Co-founder Jeffrey Raider indicated that profits from offline sales are close to those from online sales. He said that "the future of retail is a mix of online and in-store sales."[39]

Trendy eyewear retailer Warby Parker's Dave Gilboa stated:

> E-commerce is taking share but it's doing so more slowly than I think we thought when we launched...if we were just to focus on online at this time, we'd only be able to address about 3% of the overall eyewear market.

To date, they have 50 brick-and-mortar stores with 20 more to come in 2018.[40]

> **My prediction:** Brands will usually launch online and, as they gain traction, test market themselves in temporary pop-up stores. These will later be followed by in-store distribution and, in some cases, their own physical stores. Consumer brands will be omni-channel.

Consumers Will Create Their Own Preferred Paths to Purchase

The essence of omni-channel is that the consumer is in charge. Anyone who wants to purchase a product or service can research and buy what they want in whatever way they wish.

> A multitasking Parisian professional on her way home from work pulls into a suburban Carrefour hypermarket to pick up groceries, a few household items, and a birthday present for her nephew. Using the retailer's app to find the best deals, she discovers that a toy is not available in store but can be purchased online. She buys the item from the app while still in the store and elects to have it shipped there for pickup over the weekend.
>
> A shopper on Asos's fashion apparel website finds a blouse she likes but is unsure of her size. She visits a local store that

carries the same item to try it on. She completes her purchase there, but later decides she would also like the blouse in a different color. She goes to the store's website to purchase the blouse and at the same time signs up for an annual membership for free two-day shipping on all future orders.[41]

Stores, It's Time to Start Over

Omni-channel retailers, brands and consumer businesses of all kinds must re-evaluate the fundamental purpose of stores. The traditional purpose of a store, as we described in Chapter 2, was to keep an appropriate selection of inventory as close at hand as possible, serving potential customers in a market area. A store was a store-house—a 3,000-year-old business system.

But as we've seen, the internet has rendered this purpose useless, at least for many types of Mundane products. The abundance of information about products, pricing and reviews that the internet makes possible reduces the need for products to be local.

Therefore, physical retailers must ask themselves what job a consumer is "hiring" them to do in every situation.

- Are they there to offer discovery and experience for product options that consumers can later buy online?
- Are they there to provide fast, one-day, same-day or even two-hour shipping by having many local stores close to consumers?
- Are they there for consumers to shop and buy online and then pick up in the store? This option known as BOPIS (short for "buy online, pick-up in store"), also known as "click-and-collect," is becoming increasingly popular.

The purpose of stores will be to help establish a product or retailer brand in the minds of consumers, just one element of a multi-faceted branding strategy. Of course, the traditional function of stores, to transact purchases, will still be a significant part of their purpose.

> **My Prediction:** The purpose, business case and financial justification for stores, as well as the execution of physical store strategies, will be considered as part of the multiple ways consumers will want to interact with brands. Retail strategies will be analyzed around how they support the two core functions of retail: discovery and fulfillment.

Small, Fast, Fresh and Local

Fresh food, because of its perishable quality, will always need to be treated differently than other types of retailing and services, providing many opportunities for innovation. High-quality fresh food will always need to be prepared near its consumer. Whether prepared in grocery stores or restaurants, home delivery of ready-to-eat meals will increasingly be the preferred choice for busy consumers. When combined with ordering technology platforms like Grubhub, high-quality local food providers will always be a part of urban and suburban life.

There are opportunities for many new types of hybrid fresh-made, ready-to-heat-and-eat food retail formats to be developed. The word *grocerant*—the combination of grocery and restaurant describes what some of these offerings may involve.

These may combine the prepared food sections of grocery stores with an edited array of grocery products (think high-end convenience store). Or a deli might combine with a local fresh, fast, casual restaurant and include a market component for picking up a few household staples.

A part of all this will include an emphasis on locally-grown produce and regional or global cuisines. Think, mid-America comfort food as a theme—or Scandinavian, Indian or Mediterranean. Or pan-Asian noodles, sushi and stir-fry. And Italian is never going away. Did someone say "pizza"?

These concepts will leverage the fact that fresh food needs to be prepared close to the consumer. And higher-income, time-pressed suburban consumers will want the option to either have fresh food delivered or to be able to pick it up in an attractive local format that is easy to access quickly.

These formats will also leverage the fact that consumers want food that is in many stages of preparedness—from produce, meat and seafood for cooking from scratch to portioned meal kits to heat-and-eat entrées and desserts. They may want a ready-cooked entrée, but also want to throw together a quick salad or veggies in their own kitchen, and to be able to get both at the same place, quickly and easily.

These types of smaller, local formats could be developed by Amazon's Whole Foods Markets, Walmart, Target or leading convenience store chains like Sheetz and Wawa. Or they could be developed by existing restaurant companies or new start-ups.

In addition to new fresh food formats in neighborhoods and shopping centers, there is the potential for innovative fresh food concepts in alternative locations such as workplaces, colleges, hospitals and the like. If you would like to learn more about non-commercial food services, I invite you to download my free ebook introduction to the industry, called *Let's Do Lunch* at msourceideas.com/lunch.

> **My Prediction:** Fresh food, the ultimate and perennial local need, which requires a high degree of skilled labor and imagination to do well, will continue to see many varied combinations and business models in the future. As a result, it will continue to be a dynamic and fluid area for innovative new formats.

Discounts and Deals Are Always Fun

There is a huge entertainment and shopping-with-your-friends value in finding deals in physical stores. The immediate gratification of discovering a one-of-a-kind deal on an item you can take home right away cannot be replaced by online shopping.

Using our two-axis model, this type of shopping falls in the Unique zone. The uniqueness of the deal and thrill of the treasure hunt cannot be duplicated online. Flash sale websites like Zulily and Gilt that sell fashion brands at deep discounts duplicate part of the appeal of the treasure hunt, and will probably always occupy an online niche, but discount retail formats like T.J. Maxx and Marshalls will continue to thrive.

> **My Prediction:** These formats, offering the thrill of deep discounts, will remain as a strong physical retail format for a long time to come. The thrill of the treasure hunt will continue to give people a reason to leave the house.

The Future of Shopping Centers

It's time to take a closer look at the phenomenon of the enclosed shopping mall. As discussed in the previous chapter, large enclosed malls are in transition. As department store chains like Macy's, J.C. Penney and Sears close their weaker-performing stores, the malls they supported are experiencing a period of significant change.

The top-tier shopping malls located in the highest income zip codes in the U.S. have a high density of prominent store brands in the Elite and Unique categories, and continue to be vibrant and successful. The compelling concentration of sensory-rich retail along with dynamic restaurants, bars, movie theaters and other entertainment venues exert such a strong gravitational pull that these top properties will continue to be viable long into the future. In the real estate industry, these types of malls are sometimes known as "A" malls.

The next tier down, the so-called "B" malls, will need to be radically re-imagined to remain relevant. In these second-tier malls, retail uses by some department stores and clothing stores will be replaced by a greater variety of food and entertainment uses. In some cases, the operators of these "B" malls will also add creative non-retail uses such as hotels, apartments, office spaces, and gyms.

Lower-tier or "C" malls in the outer suburbs of large cities or in more rural areas will need to be even more radically re-tenanted. If they don't accomplish that, they will simply be returned to their financial lenders and altogether re-purposed. These more functional retail properties often may not be able to generate enough retail gravitation to attract foot traffic when functional shopping needs can be so easily satisfied by e-commerce.

In fact, the word "mall" is rapidly coming into disuse. Many shopping centers are now in the process of renaming their properties without the word "mall" in the name. The bland, functional shopping mall and food court surrounded by its acres of asphalt parking lots is receding into the past.

I think Victor Gruen, the Austrian architect and originator of the enclosed shopping mall, who we highlighted in Chapter 1, would be quite content to see this trend.

> **My Prediction:** Successful malls will embrace the original concept of Gruen's malls, creating an environment more integrated with the community. "A" malls will continue to be increasingly viable, while "B" malls will have to reinvent themselves to survive, and many "C" malls will disappear altogether.

The Type of Shopping Centers That Will Thrive

Let's look in more detail at what aspects of physical retail and shopping environments are likely to thrive, going forward.

In his influential 1989 book, *The Great Good Place*, which is more relevant today than ever, author Ray Oldenburg articulates the important need for a "third place" in society. The first two places being home and then work. Third places are locations like cafés, shopping arcades and other attractive central places where people can escape to relax, socialize and explore (and write books!).

Oldenburg says that these places are critical to community life and offer an important social good. He laments the relative lack of third places in the U.S., partly because of the sprawling nature of American suburbs, which often require cars to access.

He contrasts the U.S. with countries like France, Italy and Germany, which enjoy many types of third places in the form of cafés, coffee shops and beer gardens. And don't forget British pubs—my stomping grounds.

The purpose of these types of local haunts and cafés is not primarily to eat or drink, but to escape from the pressures of home and work, to socialize, to people-watch, or simply read a newspaper.

It was this idea of a third place that was Howard Schulz's chief inspiration behind his vision for Starbucks. It's not just about great coffee, but providing an attractive, local place for people to relax without pressure—a great, good place.

Shopping areas that will be relevant long into the future, even as e-commerce continues its march, will be places that are developed and orchestrated by those who deeply understand the value of their properties as third places. They will offer numerous food and beverage concepts, from restaurants, bars and cafés to grocery stores, farmers' markets, bakeries and wine shops, as well as shopping, entertainment, cultural attractions, and other types of non-commercial public spaces.

A 2014 online article published on the McKinsey consulting website stated it well.

> Online shopping provides consumers with ultimate levels of convenience. Malls will never be able to compete with the endless product selection, price comparisons and always-on nature of online. Nor should they try. Instead, malls need to move in a different direction, away from commoditized shopping experiences and toward a broadened value proposition for consumers.[42]

Shopping centers that are doing well now and that will continue to thrive in the era of unceasing adoption of e-commerce will intentionally make the shopping aspect of their properties less important.

The McKinsey article goes on to share:

> It is critical that malls be about much more than stores. We see the mix of tenant/public space moving from the current 70/30 to 60/40, or even 50/50. When this happens, these expanded public spaces will need to be planned and programmed over the year much like an exhibition. They will be managed more like content and media, instead of real estate.[43]

Retail consultant Doug Stephens has also pointed out the importance of looking at shopping malls and stores as a form of media—a way to communicate with consumers—as much as places to carry out sales transactions.[44]

Rick Caruso, the namesake and founder of Los Angeles mall developer Caruso, says that their company is not in the shopping business. Based near Hollywood, Caruso is influenced by the film industry and takes many pages from the books of films and film sets in terms of layouts, lighting and storytelling.

Caruso stated in an interview, "We're in the content and experience business... We construct narratives, scenes, feelings and moods..."[45]

Paradoxically, de-emphasizing shopping and focusing on creating a positive experiential narrative for visitors, translates directly into especially high sales. Caruso's flagship mall in Los Angeles, The Grove, has the second highest sales per square foot of all U.S. shopping malls and attracts 18 million people a year—more than Disneyland.

In addition to the movie industry cues of narrative and creating positive emotion, Rick Caruso is also heavily influenced by the hospitality industry. Caruso hires many executives from the Four Seasons hotel group, world-renowned for excelling at hospitality. He believes that retailers must also be in the hospitality business.

Shopping environments must emphasize their non-shopping appeal and have a very high level of focus on non-retail aspects to be able to continue to attract traffic. Physical retail stores and shopping centers will need to become finely tuned to create these types of experiences that online shopping can never replicate.

Successful malls offer products and shopping experiences in the Elite, Unique and Artisan quadrants of the two-axis framework, and will continue to do so. These include higher-end luxury items supported by informed sales staff—for example, the Apple store—where you can be educated to understand your purchase, as well as cars, home and personal technology, home furnishings and, of course, fashion items and accessories.

Artisan shopping experiences will include restaurants where you can meet the chef, farmers' markets where you can meet the grower, and boutiques for handcrafted items where you can get to know the craftsman.

Paco Underhill, a consultant and author of the highly-regarded book about retail *Why We Buy*, wrote about the newly opened Ponce Center in Atlanta, Georgia. This is a large urban re-development project that has transformed a red brick, 90-year-old former Sears distribution center into a maze of shops, restaurants, offices, apartments and a theme park.

Underhill describes what he calls "the New Urbanism," a reimagining of urban living that recreates the feel of a small college town without necessarily the college. New Urbanism provides an alternative to the idea of the sprawling suburbs and its need for driving everywhere. Such urban planning calls for more highly concentrated homes on small lots combined with apartments, parks and small-scale shopping that residents can walk or bike to.

Underhill writes:

> American cities are crying for reinvention. The idea that you can live, work and play in the same place is part of our tribal and villager DNA... As I have stated so often, retail and housing are intertwined concepts. The birth of the shopping mall was based on Americans moving to the suburbs. Across the world, the middle and not-so-middle class are making lifestyle and housing choices that are different from the preceding generation. It's back to the cities, and Millennials are supporting a whole host of urban work/living spaces that are curated and concierged.[46]

And:

> If asked, how many of us would choose to live, work and play in the same place? Ultimately, retail in all its forms is about supporting how we choose to live. It is the infrastructure that every urban and suburban community is built on; part provisions supply, part entertainment and reward, and originally meaningful gathering places for good neighbors.[47]

Finally, it is worth mentioning that while the U.S. is overloaded on retail real estate, many developing countries are not. In countries like India, China, Indonesia and Columbia, there are many mall and retail outlet projects still being developed. The emerging middle classes in these regions value the mall experience. In these regions, online shopping isn't developing at the same rate as in the U.S. Due to their less-developed transportation networks, fast reliable shipping is more difficult, making online shopping less convenient than here. Additionally, in some of these countries far fewer consumers own credit cards, also inhibiting e-commerce.[48]

> **My Prediction:** The type of shopping center developed in the future will integrate the experiential components that Caruso advocates. People will start to think in very different ways about what a shopping center should be. More thought will be given as to how to integrate them into the communities they are supported by. Retail developments will be woven into residential, office and community spaces to a far greater degree, as Paco Underhill prescribed above.

Automatic Replenishment of Staples

As tech retail and delivery systems improve and become more widespread, Mundane products will increasingly be purchased for home delivery or ordered online for store pick-up. This will become a routine, commoditized process using combinations of technology linking delivery services with local mass merchants and grocery stores.

Amazon is rapidly setting the standard for the near-automation of routine shopping. Other tech/retail partnerships will be developed as well, such as Google's collaboration with Walmart to compete with Amazon.

In-home voice recognition devices like Amazon Echo and Google Home may make these routine replenishment purchases very easy. Home delivery even when consumers aren't home is being made possible through services like Amazon Key. This is a web-enabled door lock that couriers can use to securely deliver products inside the customer's home.

In these ways, Mundane products, such as food staples, paper towels, toothpaste, detergent and the like, will simply flow seamlessly into people's homes.

However, Artisan products, like fresh prepared food and produce, and gourmet items, like cheese, will still provide shoppers many reasons to want to visit physical stores. There will likely be limits to the amount of personal shopping many consumers will want to simply hand over to technology companies. For example, while you are at the store shopping for Brie or a perfect avocado, why not pick up your own paper towels and toothpaste?

But it is highly likely that on some occasions and particularly during some phases of their lives, such as when they have young children or in their most advanced years, shoppers will want to delegate much of these routinized purchases to the most convenient and cost-effective providers.

> **My Prediction:** Replenishment for routine items will become partially automated, especially for certain sections of the population and at certain times of life.

Conclusion

A new medium is never an addition to an old one,
nor does it leave the old one in peace. It never
ceases to oppress the older media until it finds new
shapes and positions for them.

Marshall McLuhan

Although McLuhan was writing about the advent of TV in the above quote from 1964, his words very aptly describe how e-commerce is affecting traditional retail forms.

The medium of e-commerce will play a part of virtually every consumer shopping activity going forward. The older retail media of shops, markets and Main Streets will need to find new positions for themselves within this milieu.

Business writer Joseph Pine uses two contrasting phrases that usefully sum up the benefits to consumers of online shopping versus the benefits offered by physical retail—"time well saved" and "time well spent."[49]

Routine shopping for Mundane products handled in the most convenient way possible is time well saved and, for this, e-commerce is the perfect solution. But for products where shopping is not seen as a chore but as a reward, an escape or a social occasion, shopping will often take place in physical stores and shopping centers. In these cases, shopping is, to use Pine's phrase, time well spent.

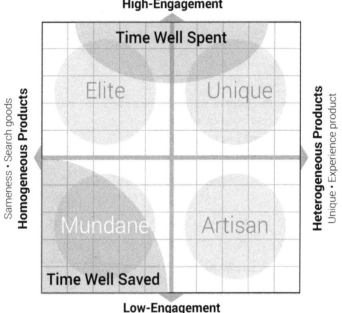

Rewarding • Shopping and Specialty product

And there is a significant gap between the two benefits. There will often be occasions where we could purchase a product online, but won't always wish to.

In the book *Wonderland: How Play Made the Modern World*, Steven Johnson writes about how our desire for play and novelty stimulated many developments in human history and created the world we live in today. Our desire for new and surprising experiences is a central feature of human nature.

> Psychologists have long understood that this appetite for surprise is an integral part of the human mind. Countless studies of newborn infants have shown that before we can crawl or grasp or communicate, we seek out surprising phenomena in our environment.[50]

We need and enjoy this stimulation of discovery and surprise and in fact, our brains are probably hard-wired for it.

> A new theory proposes that dopamine release creates a "novelty bonus" that accompanies the perception of some new phenomenon or fact about the external world. By heightening your mental faculties, making you more alert and engaged, the "novelty bonus" encourages you to learn from new experiences.[51]

It's in our nature to seek out the new—and shopping rewards this.

To revisit the quote from Jim Cramer in the Introduction… Yes, it's true. Some people may at times not wish to leave their couch—instead ordering pizza and other necessities online so they can continue playing "Call of Duty" or binging on Netflix. But at other times, they may feel summoned from home to seek surprise and delight in boldly imagined stores and retail shopping environments.

Retailers, brands and consumer businesses that understand when and why consumers want each type of experience will be those that capture shoppers' attention, minds and hearts.

Thank you for reading *The Future of Omni-Channel Retail*. If you've enjoyed reading this book, please leave a review on Amazon, Goodreads or your favorite review site. It helps me reach more people so they too can learn how to make their business relevant in the Age of Amazon.

I've been pleased to hear from various university professors that they will be using my book to explore the future of omni-channel retail in their marketing and business classes. This has also led to invitations to come speak to classes as well. If you would like to have me come speak to your class, conference or organization, you may contact me at msourceideas.com/contact.

Acknowledgments

Thank you to the following individuals, who helped me bring this book into existence, directly or indirectly.

Tara Alemany, my publisher at Emerald Lake Books. She gave me my compelling reason to forge ahead with this book—that my ideas are worth sharing—and provided excellent management, empathic guidance and careful editing very step of the way. And Mark Gerber's clever cover, illustrations and layout.

My friends, mentors, employers, bosses, clients and customers who, over the course of many business projects, have led me to unforeseen places and taught me the ideas in this book. This list includes John Hessell, Kent Trabing and John Eccleston among many others.

My friends who feign interest (just kidding!) when I tell them about my various projects, including my writing. Actually, many of them read this book and provided valuable feedback. These folks include Mark and Tamie Johnson, Pippa and Dale Hoffman, Louise and Steve Honey, Eric Wenzel, John Grapek, Vince Savage and Jack LaValley, to name a few.

My fellow writers and friends, starting with Alan Rylands and the others in his writing group: Debbie, Elisa, Robert, June, Kerry, Lorna and Marcus. They provide a fun and enthusiastic place to share ideas and validation about writing. They even provided me with good reasons to write that hadn't occurred to me. The book *If You Want to Write* by Brenda Ueland (1938) was particularly helpful. It reads as if it was written yesterday. If you've ever hesitated to write, give it a try.

I'm encouraged by people who are inspired by the challenges and possibilities of business. I've learnt from them that although business can sometimes seem too difficult, impersonal or mundane, it can also be meaningful and exhilarating, and take us to unimagined new places. Paco Underhill, Sramana Mitra, Guy Kawasaki, Tom Peters and Peter Drucker are just a few examples, as well as other authors I reference in this book.

Thanks especially to my loving and always supportive wife and young adult children. While I sometimes think they don't fully understand what I do, I can always rely on their backing and encouragement. They seem to assume I'm doing something meaningful while I'm clacking away at my laptop.

My brilliant mother Carol Binnie, who provided real support and told me that I'm "a really good writer!" And my dear father Michael Binnie, mountaineer, teacher and writer, who passed on two years ago but who would have loved to have read this. And my brother Alex and sister Katy who also cheered me along the way.

Many thanks!

About the Author

Lionel hails from the U.K. but has spent the last few decades in the U.S., first in California and later in New York, where he's now based. After working with several medium-sized retail and fashion businesses, he founded MSource Ideas, a business development consultancy in 2008.
As someone who has worked as a practitioner and consultant with consumer products and retail businesses, Lionel noticed a distinct lack of resources that tackled the questions he raises in this book. So he decided to write what was missing.

Specifically, if consumers can order virtually any product imaginable and have it delivered directly to them, what types of shopping experiences are likely to persist in the real world? And why?

Now that we are two decades into the era of e-commerce, Lionel felt we have a good vantage point to ask and answer these questions. And as someone who is intensely interested in the outcome, Lionel decided he'd tackle exploring the concept himself. This book is the result of that effort.

When he is not working as a consultant, Lionel returns quite often to England to see family—and to check whether the weather has improved. It hasn't. However, the food is getting a *lot* better.

This is Lionel's first book although he's published articles and given talks about different aspects of retail and marketing, including to The Fordham University Foundry Business Incubator, The International Conference of Shopping Centers (ICSC), and American Association of Airport Executives (AAAE).

The author enjoys connecting with his readers and can be contacted through his website at msourceideas.com.

Endnotes

1. Sax, David. *The Revenge of Analog* (New York: Hachette Book Group, 2016), 127.

2. Willsher, Kim. "Paris's Galeries de Bois, prototype of the modern shopping centre – a history of cities in 50 buildings, day 6." *The Guardian*, March 30, 2015. theguardian.com/cities/2015/mar/30/galeries-de-bois-paris-history-cities-50-buildings.

3. Johnson, Steven. *Wonderland: How Play Made the Modern World.* (New York, Riverhead Press, 2016), 42.

4. Gladwell, Malcom. "The Terrazzo Jungle." *The New Yorker.* March 15, 2004.

5. Ibid.

6. William D. Perreault, Jr., Joseph P. Cannon, E. Jerome McCarthy. *Basic Marketing, A Marketing Strategy Planning Approach, 19th Edition.* (McGraw-Hill Irwin, 2014), 197-473.

7. Christaller, Walter. Published 1933, University of Erlangen, Germany. en.wikipedia.org/wiki/Central_place_theory.

8. Goodall, B. *The Penguin Dictionary of Human Geography.* (London: Penguin. 1987).

9. Reilly, W.J. *The Law of Retail Gravitation.* (New York: Knickerbocker Press, 1931).

10. Box, George. *Statistics for Experimenters.* 2nd Edition. (Hoboken, New Jersey: John Wiley & Sons, 2005). 208, 384, and 440.

11. William D. Perreault, Jr., Joseph P. Cannon, E. Jerome McCarthy, *Basic Marketing, A Marketing Strategy Planning Approach, 19th Edition* (McGraw-Hill Irwin, 2014), 215-217.

12. Ibid, 216.

13. Nelson, Phillip. "Information and Consumer Behavior." *Journal of Political Economy 78*, no. 2 (Mar. - Apr. 1970): 311-329.

14. Zaroban, Stefany. "U.S. e-commerce Sales Grow 16% in 2017," *Digital Commerce 360.* digitalcommerce360.com/article/us-e-commerce-sales/.

15. Chaney, Sarah. "U.S. Retail Sales End 2017 on Solid Footing." *The Wall Street Journal*, January 12, 2018.

16. Keyes, Daniel. "E-Commerce will make up 17% of all US retail sales by 2022 – and one company is the main reason." *Business Insider*, August 11, 2017. businessinsider.com/e-commerce-retail-sales-2022-amazon-2017-8.

17. Carr, Austin. "The Future of Retail in the Age of Amazon." *Fast Company,* December 2017.

18. Lewis, Robin. "Retail in 2015: A Reality Check." *Forbes*, March 17, 2015. forbes.com/sites/robinlewis/2015/03/17/retail-in-2015-a-reality-check.

19. Ibid.

20. Haddon, Heather and Jargon, Julie. "Supermarkets Face a Growing Problem: Too Much Space." *The Wall Street Journal*, July 31, 2017.

21. Thomas, Lauren. "Store Closures Rocked Retail in 2017." *CNBC*. cnbc.com/2017/12/26/store-closures-rocked-retail-in-2017-and-more-should-come-next-year.html.

22. Carr, Austin. "The Future of Retail in the Age of Amazon." *Fast Company,* December 2017.

23. Kestenbaum, Richard. "There Will be More Retail Stores Opening than Closing in 2017." *Forbes.* September 11, 2017. forbes.com/sites/richardkestenbaum/2017/09/11/there-will-be-more-retail-stores-opening-than-closing-in-2017.

24. Worstall, Tim. "The Shopping Malls Really Are Being Killed by Online Shopping." *Forbes*, January 5, 2015. forbes.com/sites/timworstall/2015/01/04/the-shopping-malls-really-are-being-killed-by-online-shopping.

25. Ibid.

26. Galloway, Scott. *The Four.* (Portfolio/Penguin, New York, 2017), 44.

27. Hamstra, Mark. "Target to Buy Delivery Platform Shipt for $550M." *Supermarket News*, December 13, 2017. supermarketnews.com/online-retail/target-buy-delivery-platform-shipt-550m.

28. Jargon, Julie. "Fast-Food Chains, Upscale Restaurants Want to Bring You Lunch." *The Wall Street Journal*, June 1, 2017.

29. Mims, Christopher. "These Hot Restaurants Aren't on Maps, Only in Apps." *The Wall Street Journal*, November 5, 2017. wsj.com/articles/these-hot-restaurants-arent-on-maps-only-in-apps-1509883200.

30. Murphy, Mike. "AmazonBasics is moving well beyond the basics." *Quartz*, December 14, 2017. qz.com/1155843/amazonbasics-is-moving-well-beyond-the-basics/.

31. Safdar, Khadeeja. "Best Buy Defies Retail Doldrums, Posting Higher Sales." *The Wall Street Journal*, May 25, 2017.

32. Simon, Ruth. "7 Strategies to Loosen Amazon's Grip." *The Wall Street Journal,* August 7, 2017.

33. Ibid.

34. Ibid.

35. Ibid.

36. Ibid.

37. Ibid.

38. Brown, Eliot. "Web-Retail Startups Turn for Growth to Bricks and Mortar." *The Wall Street Journal*, May 16, 2017.

39. Ibid.

40. Ibid.

41. Ibid.

42. Fantoni, Roberto, Hoefel, Fernanda, Mazzarolo, Marina. "The Future of the Shopping Mall." *McKinsey & Company*, November 2014. mckinsey.com/business-functions/marketing-and-sales/our-insights/the-future-of-the-shopping-mall.

43. Ibid.

44. Stephens, Doug. "The Store is Media and Media is the Store." *Retail Prophet*, retailprophet.com/the-store-is-media-and-media-is-the-store/.

45. Baum, Gary. "LA's Walt Disney of Shopping." *The Hollywood Reporter*, May 21, 2015. hollywoodreporter.com/news/las-walt-disney-shopping-rick-796672.

46. Underhill, Paco. "Urban Icons in Transition." *The Robin Report*, January 9, 2018. therobinreport.com/urban-icons-in-transition/.

47. Ibid.

48. Agovino, Theresa. "Property Investors Bet on Emerging-Market Mall Culture." *The Wall Street Journal,* October 3, 2017.

49. Pine, Joseph. "Shoppers Need a Reason to Go to Your Store – Other than Buying Stuff." *The Harvard Business Review*, December 7, 2017. hbr.org/2017/12/shoppers-need-a-reason-to-go-to-your-store-other-than-buying-stuff.

50. Johnson, Steven. *Wonderland: How Play Made the Modern World.* (New York, Riverhead Press, 2016), 281.

51. Ibid.

Visit us at
emeraldlakebooks.com

CPSIA information can be obtained
at www.ICGtesting.com
Printed in the USA
BVHW09s2014200718
522152BV00010B/134/P